Stress-Free Thanksgiving

Karen Kazimer Shockley

Published by Karen's Words, 2024.

STRESS-FREE THANKSGIVING

First edition. October 19, 2024.

ISBN: 979-8231814039

Written by Karen Kazimer Shockley.

Table of Contents

My Thanksgiving Experiences

Thanksgiving is a special time for gathering with family and friends. I have many memories from different Thanksgivings. Some were more joyful, and some were more chaotic. Yet, I always enjoyed the company and the feasts. Here are some of my fondest Thanksgiving experiences.

Key West Celebrations

Many of my best Thanksgiving memories come from Key West. My in-laws owned a restaurant called "Capt. Bob's Shrimp Dock." It was a popular place. People came from all over to enjoy delicious seafood and steak. However, Thanksgiving was different. It was the only day of the year the restaurant closed.

On that day, the entire family gathered to celebrate. It felt like everyone on the island joined us. Our family would host a feast that included turkey, pototatoes, vegetables, pies, and so much more. Key Lime Pie was a must! The atmosphere was always lively.

We often had four generations of family present. There were grandparents, parents, children, and even great-grandchildren. The kids would run around, and the adults would laugh and share stories. It was a beautiful time, filled with love and laughter. Everyone helped with the cooking and the cleanup.

The Move to North Carolina

One year, we moved our Thanksgiving celebration from Key West to North Carolina. We decided to host it at a church hall. Although we were excited to continue our family tradition, things did not go as smoothly as we had hoped.

That year, we were short one turkey. We had a team of five people designated as the "Turkey Cookers." They were responsible for making sure the turkeys were cooked and ready to serve. But, of course, disaster struck. One of the designated couples forgot to turn the oven on. They didn't check the turkey for four hours. By the time we realized the problem, it was too late.

Needless to say, we had a problem. With one turkey not cooked, we had to come up with a backup plan. Luckily, we had plenty of pies to go around. We made up for the missing turkey with extra slices of pumpkin and pecan pie. In the end, we all laughed about it. The chaos made for a memorable day, even if we did not have the planned amount of turkey.

Hosting Thanksgiving

I hosted two large Thanksgivings at my house. Each time, I was told only to fix the turkey. Friends and friends brought everything else. Maybe they realized cooking was not my strong suit! I was okay with that. It took the pressure off me. I focused on the turkey while everyone else handled the side dishes and desserts.

I enjoyed having everyone at my house. The laughter, the conversations, and the food filled the rooms with joy. I loved being part of the family celebrations.

A Unique Celebration

One Thanksgiving, we visited friends instead of hosting. They had a different way of celebrating. Instead of a large feast, they served appetizers. We enjoyed various snacks, including fried bologna sandwiches. It was a fun twist on the traditional Thanksgiving meal.

We laughed and talked around the table. It was a relaxed atmosphere. The food was simple, but the company was wonderful. I realized that Thanksgiving could be celebrated in many different ways.

Meeting the Family

Another memorable Thanksgiving happened when I brought a boy home from college. He was not only my date, but it was his first time meeting my family. We went to my Aunt Betty's house, where their was room for the entire extended family.

The dining room was filled with laughter and chatter. I could tell my date was nervous. After all, he was meeting my entire family. Of course, my relatives loved to tease. They joked with him about being the oldest of fourteen kids. They must have poked fun at him at least twenty-seven times that day!

I was sure he was a bit overwhelmed. But in the end, he smiled and joined in the laughter. That's the beauty of family gatherings. They can be intense, but they can also bring everyone closer.

Thanksgivings at My Parents' House

Thanksgivings at my parents' house were always happy. My mom worked hard to prepare everything. She was an organized woman, and she liked everything to be perfect.

However, there was one thing I wished was different. I wanted to watch the Thanksgiving Day parade. I wanted to enjoy the show while preparing for dinner. My mom had a different idea. She did not believe in resting until everything was ready.

She cooked all day. The entire dinner had to be done and warming in the oven; the pots and pans had to be washed, dried, and put away before she would relax. Because of this, I often missed the parade. I would be lucky to see Santa Claus at the end of the show!

Despite this, I cherished those moments. I loved being around family, helping in the kitchen, and sharing stories. We would gather around the table and enjoy our feast together.

And later on, when my children were in their teens, we added a new tradition. The Cleveland Zoo was free on Thanksgiving Day. All of us would hurry to make sure everything was done to we could take a journey to the zoo.

The Importance of Family

Thanksgiving is a time to reflect on family and traditions. My experiences have shown me that each Thanksgiving can be different. Some gatherings are more chaotic than others, but each is filled with love.

Whether we are at my in-laws' restaurant in Key West, at a church hall in North Carolina, or in my parents' home, the spirit of Thanksgiving remains the same. It is about being together. It is about sharing food, laughter, and stories.

Every Thanksgiving has its quirks and challenges. Some years are perfect, while others are full of surprises. No matter what happens, I always find joy in the company of my loved ones. These memories shape who I am and bring warmth to my heart.

Reflecting on the Memories

As I reflect on my Thanksgiving experiences, I realize how special they are. Each story holds a piece of my heart. The laughter, the food, and the traditions bring us together.

From the bustling celebrations in Key West to the relaxed gatherings with friends, every moment matters. They teach us the value of family and friendship. They remind us to appreciate what we have and to cherish the time we spend together.

Thanksgiving is more than just a meal. It is a celebration of life, love, and gratitude. I look forward to creating more memories in the years to come. Each Thanksgiving, while we family and friends by our side, every Thanksgiving will be a success.

Thanksgiving is an opportunity to gather, reflect, and enjoy the blessings of life. In the end, it is all about connection. It is about sharing our stories and experiences with one another. As long as we have family and friends by our side, every Thanksgiving will be a success.

Chapter 1

It's a time when families and friends come together to share a meal, reflect on their blessings, and enjoy each other's company. But sometimes, in the hustle and bustle of preparing for the big day, we lose sight of what really matters. Let's take a step back and remember the true meaning of Thanksgiving.

A Brief History of Thanksgiving

The first Thanksgiving happened in 1621. The Pilgrims, who had left England to find religious freedom, settled in what is now Plymouth, Massachusetts. After a tough winter, many of them didn't survive. But with the help of the Native Americans, especially a man named Squanto, they learned how to grow crops and survive in the new land.

That fall, the Pilgrims had a successful harvest. To celebrate and give thanks, they shared a feast with the Wampanoag tribe. It wasn't just about the food—it was about gratitude. The Pilgrims were thankful for the harvest, their new friendships, and simply being alive after a year filled with hardships.

Over time, Thanksgiving became a national holiday. In 1863, President Abraham Lincoln officially declared it a day of "Thanksgiving and Praise to our beneficent Father who dwelleth in the Heavens." It was meant to be a day of reflection, a time to give thanks for what we have.

The Values of Thanksgiving: Gratitude and Togetherness

At its core, Thanksgiving is about two things: **gratitude** and **togetherness.**

Gratitude is the feeling of thankfulness. It's recognizing the good things in our lives, even if things aren't perfect. We might not always have everything we want, but Thanksgiving reminds us to focus on what we do have. Family, friends, a roof over our heads, and a meal to share—these are all blessings worth celebrating.

Togetherness is just as important. Thanksgiving is a time to gather with those we love. It's about coming together, even if it's just for a meal. Whether you're with family, friends, or neighbors, the simple act of sharing a meal brings people closer. It's not about who makes the best turkey or who brings the fanciest dessert. It's about being present with the people who matter.

Focus on Gratitude, Not Perfection

In today's world, it's easy to get caught up in making everything look perfect. We see pictures on social media of perfectly set tables, flawless meals, and smiling families. It can make us feel like our own Thanksgiving isn't good enough. But that's not what Thanksgiving is about.

The truth is, no holiday celebration is ever perfect. Maybe the turkey is a little dry, or the pie didn't come out quite right. Maybe not everyone can make it to the gathering this year. That's okay. Instead of focusing on perfection, we can choose to focus on **gratitude**.

When we focus on gratitude, we stop worrying about the little things that don't matter. We stop comparing our holiday to others. We start appreciating the simple joys—like having loved ones to share a meal with or being able to take a break from our busy lives.

Gratitude changes our perspective. It helps us see the good in everything, even when things aren't perfect. This Thanksgiving let's challenge ourselves to be grateful for what we have, instead of stressing over what we don't.

Reframe Expectations

Sometimes, the stress of hosting or attending Thanksgiving celebrations comes from unrealistic expectations. We set ourselves up for disappointment by thinking everything must go perfectly. But when we look at Thanksgiving differently, we can let go of those expectations and enjoy the day for what it is.

The Heart of Thanksgiving is Connection

The most important part of Thanksgiving isn't the food, the decorations, or even the traditions. It's the **connection**. Thanksgiving is an opportunity to connect with the people we care about. It's a chance to have meaningful conversations, laugh together, and create memories.
When we focus on connection, we realize that it doesn't matter if we remembered the cranberry sauce or if the tablecloth has a stain. What matters is the time we spend together. A heartfelt conversation is worth more than a picture-perfect meal.

Let Go of Flawless Hosting

Hosting Thanksgiving can feel overwhelming. There's so much to do—planning the menu, cooking, cleaning, decorating—it's easy to get caught up in the details. But hosting doesn't have to be stressful. In fact, it can be fun if we change how we approach it.
First, **keep things simple**. You don't have to cook everything from scratch or have an elaborate spread. Choose a few key dishes that you love to make, and don't be afraid to ask for help. Guests are usually happy

to bring a side dish or dessert. The meal doesn't have to be fancy to be memorable.

Second, **relax your standards**. It's okay if the house isn't spotless or if the decorations are minimal. What matters is the feeling of warmth and welcome. Your guests will remember how they felt in your home, not whether the centerpiece was perfect.

Lastly, **enjoy the process**. Cooking can be a fun activity, especially when done with others. Invite family or friends into the kitchen to help. It turns a chore into quality time.

Enjoy the Day, No Matter What

Sometimes, things go wrong. Maybe the turkey burns, or a family member is running late. Maybe there's a bit of tension or disagreement at the dinner table. These things happen. But they don't have to ruin the day.

When we let go of the idea that everything must be perfect, we open ourselves up to enjoying the moment, no matter what happens. Thanksgiving isn't about everything going according to plan. It's about **being present**. It's about **embracing the imperfections** and finding joy in the unexpected.

If something goes wrong, laugh it off. Every Thanksgiving has its mishaps, and those mishaps often become the stories we tell and laugh about later. The key is to stay flexible and focus on what really matters—the people we're with and the gratitude in our hearts.

Finding Joy in the Simple Moments

At the end of the day, Thanksgiving is a time to pause and reflect. It's a chance to be thankful for the simple, often overlooked blessings in our lives. It's a time to enjoy the company of those we care about, without worrying about perfection or expectations.

This year let's focus on the true meaning of Thanksgiving. Let's embrace the values of gratitude and togetherness. Let's let go of the pressure to have everything just right and instead focus on creating meaningful, joyful moments.

Thanksgiving is about connection, not perfection. It's about gratitude, not stress. And when we approach it with that mindset, we can find peace, joy, and fulfillment, no matter what the day brings.

Let's make this Thanksgiving a celebration of what truly matters—love, gratitude, and the people we cherish.

Chapter 2

Thanksgiving is a wonderful holiday, but it can feel overwhelming. The key to reducing stress is simple: plan. By breaking things down and getting organized early, you can avoid the last-minute rush and enjoy the day. Let's dive into some easy ways to prepare.

Create a Clear, Simple Game Plan

The first step to a stress-free Thanksgiving is creating a game plan. Think of it as your road map to the holiday. It doesn't have to be complicated—just a simple outline of what needs to happen and when.

1. Start Early
   Don't wait until the week of Thanksgiving to start planning. A few weeks ahead of time is the perfect moment to begin. This gives you enough time to think things through without feeling rushed.

2. Create a Guest List
   Who's coming to your Thanksgiving meal? This is one of the first questions to answer. Write down your guest list. Knowing how many people to expect helps with planning the menu and seating. It's also a good idea to confirm with your guests about two weeks before Thanksgiving so there are no surprises.

3. Plan the Menu
   Once you know how many people are coming, it's time to plan the menu. Keep it simple. You don't need to have 10 different side dishes or 5 types of pie. Stick with the basics: turkey, a

couple of side dishes, and dessert. It's okay to add one or two extras if you're feeling up for it, but don't overdo it. Focus on making the meal enjoyable, not complicated.

A traditional Thanksgiving menu might include turkey, mashed potatoes, stuffing, green beans, cranberry sauce, and pumpkin pie. That's enough to make most people happy. If you have guests with dietary restrictions, try to accommodate them, but keep it simple. You can add a vegetarian or gluten-free option, but there's no need to reinvent the entire menu.

1. Make a Shopping List
    After you've planned your menu, make a detailed shopping list. Go through each recipe and write down the ingredients you'll need. This helps you avoid multiple trips to the store. Be sure to include any special items you might need, like turkey basters or extra serving dishes. Organize your list by category (produce, dairy, etc.) to make shopping easier.

2. Shop Early
    Don't wait until the day before Thanksgiving to do your shopping. Get non-perishable items, like canned goods or baking supplies, a week or two ahead. Fresh ingredients, like vegetables and turkey, can be bought a few days before the holiday. By spreading out your shopping, you'll avoid the stress of last-minute crowds.

3. Set the Table in Advance
    If you're hosting a larger gathering, set the table the night before. This is one less thing to worry about on Thanksgiving Day. Lay out the plates, silverware, glasses, and napkins. You can even add any decorative touches, like candles or centerpieces, ahead of time.

Set Realistic Goals

A big part of staying stress-free is setting realistic goals. It's easy to get caught up in wanting everything to be perfect, but that can lead to unnecessary pressure. Thanksgiving is about being with loved ones, not about having a flawless event.

1. Know Your Limits
    Everyone has different skills and time limits. Be honest with yourself about what you can handle. Maybe you're not great at baking, or you don't enjoy cooking all day. That's okay. You don't have to do everything yourself. Know what your strengths are and focus on them. If you're great at making the turkey but don't enjoy baking pies, consider buying dessert from a bakery or asking a guest to bring it.

2. Simplify Where You Can
    Thanksgiving doesn't have to be a fancy, over-the-top affair. Simplify wherever possible. Maybe that means serving fewer side dishes or using store-bought items for part of the meal. For example, instead of making everything from scratch, you can use pre-made pie crusts or boxed stuffing mix. The goal is to make the day enjoyable for you and your guests, not to impress anyone with your cooking skills.

3. Prioritize What Matters Most
    Focus on what's most important to you. Is it spending time with family? Having a delicious meal? Enjoying a cozy, relaxed atmosphere? Prioritize those things and let go of the rest. For example, if you love spending time around the table with the family, make sure you leave enough time to sit and enjoy the meal. Don't spend the whole day in the kitchen.

4. Expect Things to Go Wrong
    No matter how much you plan, something might go wrong. The turkey might take longer to cook than expected, or a side

dish might not turn out right. That's okay. It's all part of the experience. Instead of stressing over small mishaps, embrace them as part of the day. Remember, the true spirit of Thanksgiving is about being thankful, not about everything being perfect.

Delegate Tasks to Reduce Stress

One of the best ways to reduce stress is by delegating tasks. You don't have to do everything yourself. Thanksgiving is about coming together, and that includes working together. Here's how to get others involved.

1. Ask for Help Early
   Don't wait until the last minute to ask for help. If you need someone to bring a dish or help with cooking, ask them ahead of time. Most people are happy to contribute, but they'll appreciate the advance notice. It's also a good idea to assign tasks based on people's strengths. For example, if your sister loves baking, ask her to bring dessert. If your friend is great at setting up, let them handle the decorations.
2. Delegate Cooking
   If you're hosting a large group, there's no need to cook everything yourself. Assign different dishes to different people. For example, you can cook the turkey but ask guests to bring side dishes or appetizers. This not only reduces your workload but also adds variety to the meal.
3. Get Family Members Involved
   Thanksgiving is a family holiday, so get everyone involved. Even kids can help out in simple ways, like setting the table or stirring ingredients. If you have older kids or teens, ask them to take on bigger tasks, like washing dishes or helping with prep work. Spreading out the responsibilities helps everyone feel involved and makes the day run more smoothly.

4. Delegate Cleanup
    Don't take on all the cleanup yourself. After the meal, ask guests to help clear the table and wash dishes. You can even make it fun by turning on some music or offering small desserts while cleaning up. When everyone pitches in, cleanup becomes less of a burden.

5. Plan Non-Cooking Tasks
    Delegating isn't just about food. There are other tasks that need to be handled, too. For example, ask someone to oversee seating arrangements or decorating the table. You can also assign someone to manage any games or activities, like a Thanksgiving trivia quiz or a family walk after the meal.

6. Use Time-Saving Tools
    Another way to reduce stress is by using time-saving tools in the kitchen. Consider using a slow cooker for certain dishes, like mashed potatoes or stuffing. A slow cooker keeps food warm and frees up space on the stove. You can also use disposable dishes for certain parts of the meal, which makes cleanup easier.

A Thanksgiving to Remember

Thanksgiving is meant to be a joyful time, not a stressful one. By planning ahead, setting realistic goals, and delegating tasks, you can reduce the pressure and focus on what really matters: enjoying the holiday with your loved ones.

Creating a clear game plan helps keep things organized and ensures you're not scrambling at the last minute. Setting realistic goals allows you to enjoy the process without aiming for perfection. And delegating tasks spreads out the work and makes the day more enjoyable for everyone.

This year, instead of worrying about everything being perfect, focus on the spirit of Thanksgiving. Appreciate the moments of togetherness, the laughter, and the joy of sharing a meal. When you do that, you'll find that Thanksgiving becomes a day to truly be thankful for.

Chapter 3

Thanksgiving dinner is often seen as the highlight of the holiday. But planning the meal can be stressful, especially if you're trying to juggle a bunch of different dishes, dietary restrictions, and time constraints. The good news is you don't have to be overwhelmed. With a manageable menu, some practical recipes, and a little planning, you can put together a delicious Thanksgiving meal without the chaos.

Crafting a Manageable Menu

When it comes to Thanksgiving, it's easy to get carried away with all the traditional dishes. But that doesn't mean you have to make everything. In fact, trying to recreate an elaborate feast with ten different sides, three desserts, and a giant turkey can be exhausting. Instead, focus on crafting a menu that works for you.

Stick to the Basics

Start with the core of the meal. For most families, that's turkey, mashed potatoes, stuffing, and maybe a few side dishes. You don't need to go overboard. A simple, well-cooked meal will be more enjoyable than a complicated one that stresses you out.

Think about the traditional dishes that matter most to your family. Maybe it's green bean casserole or cranberry sauce. Whatever it is, prioritize those dishes, and let the rest go. This is about creating a meal that you'll enjoy making and eating, not about competing with a food magazine.

Limit the Number of Dishes

Keep it manageable by limiting the number of dishes you're preparing. You don't need six different kinds of vegetables, three pies, or four variations of stuffing. A well-rounded meal can be achieved with just a few carefully chosen dishes.

For example, you can plan on turkey, mashed potatoes, a vegetable side, stuffing, and a pie. That's enough variety to keep everyone happy, but it won't overwhelm you in the kitchen. If you want to offer something extra, add a simple salad or an easy appetizer like cheese and crackers.

Practical Recipes

Use recipes that are practical and time-saving. Not everything has to be made from scratch, especially if it's going to stress you out. Consider using shortcuts, like pre-made pie crusts or store-bought rolls. These little time-savers can make a big difference in your stress level.

Focus on recipes you know well. Thanksgiving is not the time to try an elaborate new dish. Stick with recipes you're comfortable with and that have worked in the past. If you want to try something new, make sure it's simple and not too time-consuming.

Balance Tradition with Ease

If you feel tied to traditional dishes, balance them with easy options. For instance, you might make traditional stuffing from scratch but opt for canned cranberry sauce. The goal is to have a nice mix of homemade dishes and time-savers, so you don't feel overwhelmed.

Thanksgiving is all about comfort and connection, not perfection. The meal should be enjoyable, not stressful. Keeping things simple will help you enjoy the day.

Accommodating Dietary Needs Without Stress

These days, it's common to have guests with dietary restrictions. Whether it's vegetarian, gluten-free, or something else, accommodating special diets can seem daunting. But it doesn't have to be.

Don't Overcomplicate It

First of all, don't feel like you have to make separate meals for everyone. You can accommodate most dietary needs with a few simple adjustments to your menu. Instead of making two versions of everything, think about what dishes can be easily adapted.

For example, if you have a vegetarian guest, you don't need to create a whole new meal. Offer a few sides that don't contain meat, like mashed potatoes, roasted vegetables, or a salad. You can also make a vegetarian stand-alone stuffing by using vegetable broth instead of chicken broth.

Make Simple Substitutions

Many traditional dishes can be made to accommodate special diets with simple substitutions. For instance, if you have a guest who is gluten-free, you can use gluten-free bread in your stuffing. If someone is lactose intolerant, you can use dairy-free butter in your mashed potatoes.

These small adjustments are often all you need to make sure everyone can enjoy the meal without feeling left out. Don't feel like you need to reinvent the entire menu for dietary restrictions. Just focus on making a few key dishes accessible to all your guests.

Ask Your Guests for Input

If you're unsure about how to accommodate a guest's dietary needs, don't be afraid to ask. Your guests will appreciate that you're trying to make them comfortable, and they might even offer to bring a dish that fits their diet.

For example, if you have a vegan guest, ask them what their favorite Thanksgiving dish is and how they usually make it. You might discover a great new recipe to try. At the same time, it takes some of the pressure off you to figure it all out on your own.

Offer a Variety of Options

One of the easiest ways to accommodate different diets is by offering a variety of dishes. If you have a mix of vegetarians and meat-eaters, offer a few sides that can serve as a main dish for your vegetarian guests.

For example, roasted vegetables, sweet potato casserole, and a hearty salad can all be substantial enough for vegetarians without adding extra work for you. The key is to offer enough options so that everyone has something to enjoy.

Considering Make-Ahead Dishes

One of the best ways to reduce stress on Thanksgiving Day is by preparing dishes ahead of time. Make-ahead dishes save you time and allow you to enjoy the holiday without being stuck in the kitchen all day.

Choose Dishes That Hold Up Well

Not every dish is suited for making ahead of time, but many Thanksgiving classics are. Casseroles, pies, and stuffing can all be prepared the day before and reheated on Thanksgiving Day. This frees up time and space in the kitchen, making the day feel less hectic.

When planning your menu, think about which dishes can be made ahead. Mashed potatoes, for example, can be prepped the day before and reheated in the oven or slow cooker. Gravy can also be made ahead and reheated before serving.

Prep Ingredients in Advance

Even if you can't make an entire dish ahead of time, you can still prepare ingredients in advance. Chop vegetables, peel potatoes, and measure out ingredients the day before. This way, when it's time to cook, everything is ready to go.

You can also prepare pie crusts ahead of time or even bake your pies a day in advance. Desserts tend to hold up well, so you can get them out of the way early. Plus, this gives you one less thing to worry about on Thanksgiving Day.

Reheat with Care

When reheating make-ahead dishes, be mindful of how they hold up. Some dishes, like casseroles, reheat beautifully, while others may need a little extra attention. If you're reheating mashed potatoes, for example, you may need to add a splash of milk or butter to keep them creamy.

Make sure to plan for reheating time in your schedule. If you're using the oven to reheat multiple dishes, you may need to stagger the timing or use different appliances, like a slow cooker or microwave, to keep everything warm.

Consider Freezing

Some dishes can even be made weeks in advance and frozen. Pies, casseroles, and rolls are all great candidates for freezing.

If you're feeling ambitious, make a few dishes a couple of weeks before Thanksgiving and freeze them. Then, all you need to do is defrost and reheat them on the big day.

This can be a huge time-saver, especially if you're hosting a large group. Just make sure to thaw frozen dishes in the refrigerator the day before Thanksgiving, so they're ready to go when you need them.

A Menu That Works for You

Planning a Thanksgiving menu doesn't have to be stressful. By keeping things simple, accommodating dietary needs with small adjustments, and preparing dishes in advance, you can enjoy a delicious meal without the overwhelm.

Remember, Thanksgiving is about more than just the food. It's about gathering with loved ones, sharing gratitude, and creating lasting memories. By crafting a manageable menu, you can focus on what really matters: spending time with the people you care about.

So, this year, let go of the pressure to create a perfect feast. Stick to the basics, keep it simple, and enjoy the holiday for what it truly is: a time to connect, reflect, and give thanks.

Chapter 4

Shopping for Thanksgiving can feel like a daunting task. With so many ingredients to buy and a long list of things to remember, it's easy to feel overwhelmed. But it doesn't have to be stressful. With a little planning and some smart strategies, you can get all the shopping done efficiently and with minimal hassle. In this chapter, we'll look at how to create a detailed shopping list, time your shopping trips, and explore the benefits of using online grocery services.

Creating a Detailed Shopping List

The first step to stress-free shopping is creating a solid, organized shopping list. If you're planning your Thanksgiving meal, it's important to know exactly what you'll need, and breaking it down into categories can make the process smoother.

1. **Start Early**

   Begin by making your menu. Once you know what dishes you're serving, go through each recipe and write down every ingredient. It helps to do this well in advance, so you can avoid the last-minute scramble. This way, you'll have plenty of time to check your pantry for items you already have and avoid buying duplicates.

2. **Organize by Category**

   Once you have your list of ingredients, group them into categories like produce, dairy, meats, canned goods, and baking supplies. This makes your trip to the store much more efficient because you'll know exactly where to go. No more zigzagging across the store trying to remember what you need!

Here's how you can break it down:

- **Produce**: Potatoes, onions, carrots, celery, etc.
- **Dairy**: Butter, cream, milk, eggs.
- **Meats**: Turkey, sausage (if making stuffing), ham.
- **Canned/Baking**: Cranberry sauce, canned pumpkin, broth, flour, sugar, etc.

Organizing your list this way helps you avoid forgetting things and limits how much time you spend wandering the aisles.

1. **Check Your Kitchen**
   Before heading to the store, take a quick inventory of your kitchen. You might already have some items in your pantry or fridge. Cross those off your list. This step not only saves you money but also helps prevent clutter by reducing unnecessary items.
2. **Be Specific**
   When making your list, be as specific as possible. If a recipe calls for a particular type of ingredient, write that down. For example, if you need unsalted butter or a specific type of spice, make sure it's clear on your list. This can save you from having to run back to the store later.

Strategic Timing for Shopping Trips

Timing is key when it comes to stress-free holiday shopping. Knowing when to shop can make a huge difference in your overall experience.

Shop Early

One of the easiest ways to reduce stress is by shopping early. Don't wait until the day before Thanksgiving to get all your groceries. Stores are often packed during the days leading up to the holiday, and the last thing you want is to be stuck in long lines or finding out they're out of key ingredients.

Aim to do your main grocery shopping about a week before Thanksgiving. By then, stores are typically well-stocked, and you'll beat the worst of the crowds. You can always make a quick trip for any last-minute items a couple of days before, but getting the bulk of your shopping done early will save you a lot of headaches.

Go During Off-Peak Hours

If you're able to, try shopping during off-peak hours. Early mornings or late evenings tend to be quieter times at grocery stores. Avoid the lunch rush or evenings right after work when stores are busier.

Weekdays are also generally less crowded than weekends, so if you have the flexibility to shop on a weekday morning or afternoon, take advantage of it. The calmer the store, the quicker and more pleasant your shopping experience will be.

Break Up Your Shopping

You don't have to get everything in one trip. If the idea of doing all your shopping in one go feels overwhelming, try breaking it up into two or three smaller trips. For example, you can shop for non-perishable items (like canned goods, spices, and baking supplies) a couple of weeks ahead of time. Then, closer to Thanksgiving, you can shop for perishable items like fresh vegetables, dairy, and meats.

Breaking it up also means you're less likely to forget something, and it helps you feel more in control of the process.

Have a Backup Plan

Sometimes, stores run out of popular items right before the holiday. If this happens, don't panic. Having a backup plan can save you a lot of stress. For example, if you can't find fresh cranberries, have a canned option on hand. Or if the specific brand of turkey you want is sold out, be flexible with your choices. Knowing that you have alternatives will help you stay calm even if things don't go perfectly.

Using Online Grocery Services

In recent years, online grocery shopping has become more popular, and it's a fantastic way to save time and reduce stress during the holiday season. Here's why you should consider using grocery delivery or curbside pickup services for Thanksgiving.

Convenience

One of the biggest benefits of online grocery shopping is the convenience. Instead of navigating a crowded store, you can do all your shopping from the comfort of your home. Most online grocery platforms allow you to search for items, compare prices, and add things to your cart at your own pace. It's a stress-free alternative to in-store shopping.

Many grocery stores now offer both delivery and curbside pickup options, so you can choose whichever is most convenient for you. Delivery saves you a trip to the store altogether, while curbside pickup lets you avoid going inside, but still allows you to get your groceries when it's convenient for you.

Save Time

Shopping online can save you a lot of time, especially during the busy holiday season. Instead of spending hours at the grocery store, you can quickly find what you need online and have it delivered or ready for pickup in a matter of hours.

With curbside pickup, all you have to do is drive to the store, and they'll bring the groceries right out to your car. It's an easy way to get everything you need without having to deal with the hassle of parking, lines, or crowds.

Reduce Impulse Buys

One of the advantages of shopping online is that it helps you stick to your list. When you're in a store, it's easy to get tempted by impulse buys—things you didn't plan on getting but grabbed because they looked good in the moment. With online shopping, you're more likely to focus on the items you need, which can help you stay within your budget and avoid clutter.

Price Comparisons

Another benefit of online grocery shopping is the ability to compare prices easily. Most platforms show you the price of each item, and some even let you see discounts or alternative brands. This can help you save money and choose the best options for your budget.

Customizing Your Order

Most online grocery services allow you to customize your order. You can choose specific quantities, make notes for the store (like asking for the ripest avocados or a specific size of turkey), and even substitute items if something is out of stock.

Many services also allow you to schedule your delivery or pickup in advance, so you can choose a time that works best for you. This flexibility makes it easier to plan around your schedule and avoid last-minute rushes.

Reduce Holiday Stress

Thanksgiving can be a hectic time, and any tool that reduces stress is worth considering. Using online grocery services means you won't have to fight the crowds or deal with the chaos of the store right before a major holiday. You can order what you need, relax, and know that your groceries will be ready when you are.

Shopping Without Stress

Shopping for Thanksgiving doesn't have to be a stressful experience. With a detailed shopping list, smart timing, and the option of using online grocery services, you can make the process smooth and manageable.

By planning ahead and using tools to simplify the experience, you'll save time, avoid the last-minute rush, and be able to focus on what really matters: spending time with loved ones and enjoying the holiday.

Remember, it's not about getting everything perfect—it's about making the holiday enjoyable for you and your family. Taking control of your shopping process is a great way to reduce stress and embrace the true spirit of Thanksgiving.

Chapter 5

The day before Thanksgiving is an important time to get ready. Preparing in advance can make the holiday feel smoother and more enjoyable. You want to avoid feeling rushed or overwhelmed on the big day, and one of the best ways to do that is to take care of as much as possible the day before. In this chapter, we'll talk about kitchen prep tips, managing time and space, and how to keep things calm and organized in the kitchen.

Final Kitchen Prep Tips

Getting everything ready the night before Thanksgiving is key to feeling relaxed and prepared. There are some simple steps you can take to make sure you're ready to cook and enjoy the holiday.

Prepare Your Ingredients Early

One of the easiest ways to save time on Thanksgiving Day is to get your ingredients ready in advance. If you can, chop vegetables, peel potatoes, and measure spices the night before. Store everything in containers or plastic bags in the fridge, so when you start cooking, everything is ready to go.

This saves you time on Thanksgiving morning, and you won't have to rush to get everything done at once. Plus, your kitchen will feel more organized because you'll have less clutter to deal with.

Setting the Table in Advance

Setting the table the night before is another great way to reduce stress. Lay out the plates, utensils, napkins, and glasses so that's one less thing to worry about. If you're planning to use special dishes or decorations, take them out the night before and make sure everything is clean and ready to go.

You can even write out place cards if you want assigned seating, or make sure you have enough chairs for everyone. Doing these small tasks early will give you more time to focus on cooking and spending time with your guests on Thanksgiving Day.

Organize Your Cookware and Tools

The night before Thanksgiving is the perfect time to organize your kitchen tools and cookware. Take out all the pots, pans, and utensils you'll need and place them near the stove or on the counter. If you need a roasting pan for the turkey or a special dish for your stuffing, have it ready and within reach.

This way, you won't be scrambling to find things when it's time to start cooking. You'll know exactly where everything is, which makes the process smoother and more enjoyable.

Check the Recipes

If you're following recipes, take a few minutes the night before to read through them again. Make sure you know the steps and have all the ingredients. This helps avoid any surprises on Thanksgiving Day, like missing ingredients or steps you didn't notice before.

Managing Time and Space

Cooking a big meal like Thanksgiving dinner can be tricky, especially when it comes to managing your time and space. But with a little planning, you can make the process feel more organized and calm.

Create a Cooking Schedule

A great way to manage your time is by creating a cooking schedule. Think about how long each dish will take to cook and plan out what time you need to start each one. For example, if the turkey takes four hours to cook, you'll want to make sure it goes into the oven with enough time to be ready before dinner.

Make a list of each dish you're preparing and write down what time you need to start cooking it. You can also note what time things will be done, so you know when to move them out of the oven or off the stove.

Use Your Space Wisely

Kitchens can feel small, especially when you're cooking a lot of dishes at once. One way to reduce stress is by using your space wisely. Clear off any unnecessary clutter from your counters and make sure you have plenty of room to work.

If you have limited counter space, consider setting up a separate area for things like chopping vegetables or mixing ingredients. This could be a small table or even part of the dining room table. The more space you have to work, the less crowded the kitchen will feel.

Delegate Tasks

You don't have to do everything yourself! Thanksgiving is about coming together with family and friends, so don't be afraid to ask for help. Whether it's setting the table, chopping vegetables, or stirring a pot, there are plenty of tasks you can delegate to others.

If someone offers to help, take them up on it. Even simple tasks like pouring drinks or arranging appetizers can make a big difference. The more hands you have helping, the more relaxed you'll feel.

Stagger the Cooking

You don't have to cook everything at once. In fact, it's better if you stagger the cooking process to keep things under control. Start with the dishes that take the longest to cook, like the turkey or casseroles, and work your way to the quicker items like rolls or side dishes.

This helps keep the kitchen organized and prevents too many things from happening at once. Plus, it ensures that all the food will be hot and ready at the same time when it's time to eat.

Reducing Kitchen Chaos

Thanksgiving cooking doesn't have to feel chaotic. By staying organized and following a few simple tips, you can keep the kitchen tidy and calm, even as you prepare a big meal.

1. **Clean as You Go**
   One of the best ways to keep your kitchen under control is to clean as you go. Instead of letting dishes, pots, and utensils pile up, take a few minutes to wash them or put them in the dishwasher as you finish using them.

For example, if you finish chopping vegetables, wash the cutting board and knife right away. If a pot is empty, clean it or at least rinse it out. Keeping the sink and counters clear will make the kitchen feel less cluttered, and it will save you from having a mountain of dishes to clean after dinner.

1. **Use Trash Bowls or Bins**
   When you're prepping ingredients, like peeling potatoes or chopping vegetables, it helps to have a designated trash bowl or bin nearby. Instead of walking back and forth to the trash can or compost bin, you can throw all the scraps in one bowl and empty it later.

This keeps your workspace clean and organized, and it saves time because you won't have to stop and clean up every few minutes. Plus, it helps reduce the mess on your counters, which can help you stay focused on cooking.

Keep Tools Handy

Another way to reduce chaos in the kitchen is by keeping your tools close at hand. If you're using a whisk, spatula, or measuring cups, keep them nearby instead of putting them back in a drawer after each use. This saves time and makes cooking feel more efficient.

You can place tools in a container on the counter or lay them on a clean towel nearby. Just make sure you have everything you need within arm's reach, so you don't have to stop and look for things while you cook.

Take Breaks

Cooking a big meal can be tiring, so don't forget to take breaks. If you feel yourself getting overwhelmed or tired, step away from the kitchen for a few minutes. Take a short walk, stretch, or sit down and enjoy a glass of water or tea.

Giving yourself a mental and physical break can help reduce stress and prevent burnout. Plus, stepping away from the kitchen can give you a chance to recharge and refocus, so you'll feel more organized when you come back.

Wrapping Up

The day before Thanksgiving is all about getting everything ready, so the holiday itself feels relaxed and enjoyable. By preparing ingredients, organizing your space, and creating a cooking schedule, you can set yourself up for success. Remember to delegate tasks, use your space wisely, and keep the kitchen tidy as you cook.

The key to reducing stress is staying organized and focusing on what matters most: spending time with your loved ones and enjoying the holiday. When the day is over, you'll feel proud of the delicious meal you've prepared and the memories you've created with family and friends.

Thanksgiving is a time to come together and be grateful, not just for the food, but for the love and support of the people around you. Preparing the day before ensures that you can enjoy that time without feeling overwhelmed or rushed. With a little planning, your Thanksgiving can be a success, and your kitchen can remain calm, even while you're cooking up a storm.

Chapter 6

Thanksgiving Day has finally arrived! It's an exciting time filled with family, food, and fun. But it can also feel overwhelming. With a house full of people and a big meal to prepare, it's easy to get caught up in the chaos. This chapter will help you stay calm and enjoy the day. We'll cover a morning routine to start your day right, time management tips for cooking, and how to be flexible when things don't go as planned.

Morning Routine for a Relaxed Thanksgiving

Starting your day with a peaceful mindset is important. A relaxed morning can set the tone for the entire day. Here are some tips to help you get started.

1. **Wake Up Early**
   Give yourself extra time in the morning. Set your alarm for at least an hour earlier than usual. This way, you can enjoy some quiet time before the hustle and bustle begins. You can sip coffee or tea and take a moment to breathe deeply.

2. **Enjoy a Simple Breakfast**
   Have a light breakfast to fuel your body. You don't want to feel hungry while cooking. Think about having something easy like yogurt with fruit, oatmeal, or toast. This will give you the energy you need without feeling too full.

3. **Take a Few Minutes for Yourself**
   After breakfast, spend a few minutes doing something you enjoy. Whether it's reading a few pages of a book, doing a quick

meditation, or taking a short walk, find a way to center yourself. This time can help clear your mind and reduce stress.

4. **Set Realistic Expectations**
Remember that Thanksgiving is about connection, not perfection. Set realistic expectations for the day. Accept that things might not go exactly as planned. That's okay! Focus on enjoying the moments with your loved ones instead of striving for a flawless event.

5. **Visualize the Day**
Spend a moment visualizing how you want the day to unfold. Picture the laughter, the conversations, and the joy of being together. This positive visualization can help you approach the day with a calm and open mindset.

Time Management Tips for Cooking on Schedule

With a busy day ahead, managing your time is crucial. Here are some tips to help you stay on schedule while cooking.

1. **Refer to Your Cooking Schedule**
Remember the cooking schedule you created the day before? Keep it handy in the kitchen. As you start cooking, refer to it often. This will help you stay on track and remind you what to cook next.

2. **Stagger Cooking Times**
Not all dishes need to be cooked at the same time. Stagger your cooking times to manage your workload. Start with the longest-cooking items, like the turkey, and work your way to the quicker ones, such as rolls or desserts.

For example, if your turkey takes four hours to cook, put it in the oven first. While it's cooking, you can prepare side dishes like stuffing or mashed potatoes.

1. **Use Timers**

    Set timers for everything! It's easy to lose track of time when you're busy in the kitchen. Timers can help remind you when to check on the food or when to start preparing the next dish. You can use kitchen timers, your phone, or even a smart speaker to set reminders.

2. **Keep the Kitchen Organized**

    As you cook, keep the kitchen organized. Put away ingredients and tools as you finish using them. This prevents clutter and makes it easier to find what you need. An organized space helps you stay focused and reduces stress.

3. **Prep Ahead for Shortcuts**

    If you have some dishes that can be cooked or prepared ahead of time, take advantage of that. For example, if you made some side dishes the day before, just pop them in the oven to heat. This gives you more time to focus on the main course and other tasks.

Being Flexible with the Timeline

Even with the best plans, things don't always go smoothly. Being flexible is key to staying calm. Here's how to handle unexpected situations.

1. **Expect the Unexpected**

    Accept that things might not go as planned. The turkey could take longer to cook, or a dish might burn. Instead of panicking, take a deep breath. Stay calm and remind yourself that it's all part of the day.

2. **Adjust as Needed**

    If you find that your cooking times are off, adjust your plan. If the turkey takes longer, it's okay to move side dishes to a later time. You can always serve dishes later or adjust cooking times. Just keep an eye on the overall timeline.

3. **Ask for Help**

   If things start to feel overwhelming, don't hesitate to ask for help. Family members or friends can pitch in. They can stir pots, set the table, or prepare appetizers. It's okay to lean on others when you need support.

4. **Stay Positive**

   Maintain a positive attitude. Laugh off any mishaps and don't dwell on them. Instead, focus on the joy of being with your loved ones. If a dish doesn't turn out as expected, turn it into a funny story to share later.

5. **Take Breaks**

   If you feel overwhelmed, step away for a moment. Take a short break to breathe and regroup. A quick walk or even a few minutes of stretching can help clear your mind and refocus your energy.

6. **Let Go of Perfection**

   Remember, Thanksgiving is about being together, not about having everything perfect. If something doesn't go as planned, let it go. Your guests are there to enjoy the time with you, not just the food. Keep the focus on the fun, laughter, and gratitude.

Enjoying the Process

Amid all the cooking and preparation, it's important to enjoy the process. Here's how to make the most of your Thanksgiving Day.

1. **Savor the Moments**

   Take time to savor the moments throughout the day. Enjoy the smell of the turkey cooking and the laughter of family members. Don't rush through the day. Pause to appreciate the little things.

2. **Engage with Your Guests**

Spend time talking and engaging with your guests as they arrive. Don't get so caught up in cooking that you forget to connect with them. Share stories, catch up, and enjoy each other's company.

3. **Create Family Traditions**
   Thanksgiving is a great time to create family traditions. Whether it's a special toast, a group photo, or sharing what you're thankful for, these traditions help strengthen family bonds. They also make the day more memorable.

4. **Enjoy the Meal Together**
   When it's time to sit down for the meal, take a moment to appreciate the spread before you. Enjoy the beautiful table setting and the delicious food. Encourage everyone to share what they are thankful for before diving into the meal.

5. **Reflect on Gratitude**
   After the meal, take a moment to reflect on gratitude. Thanksgiving is about coming together and giving thanks. Spend some time sharing stories or memories that highlight what you appreciate about each other.

6. **Plan for Relaxation**
   After all the hard work, plan for some relaxation time. Whether it's enjoying dessert, playing games, or watching a movie, make space to unwind. This helps everyone transition from the busy meal to a more relaxed atmosphere.

Wrapping Up

Thanksgiving Day can be a whirlwind of activity, but it can also be a day of joy and connection. By starting your morning with a peaceful routine, managing your time effectively, and being flexible with unexpected changes, you can enjoy the holiday to the fullest.

Remember, the heart of Thanksgiving is not just about the meal but about being with the people you love. Embrace the joy, laughter, and gratitude that fills the day. When you focus on connection rather than perfection, you create lasting memories that everyone will cherish.

So, take a deep breath, enjoy the process, and make this Thanksgiving a day to remember!

Chapter 7

Hosting Thanksgiving can be a lot of fun, but it can also feel overwhelming. The key is to create a warm, inviting atmosphere where everyone feels welcome. This chapter will help you set the stage for a fantastic Thanksgiving. We'll explore simple decorating ideas, engaging activities for your guests, and tips for handling unexpected situations with grace.

Creating a Warm, Inviting Atmosphere

A warm atmosphere makes all the difference. It helps guests feel at home. Here are some easy ways to create that inviting vibe.

1. **Set the Scene with Simple Decor**
   You don't need to go overboard with decorations. A few thoughtful touches can create a welcoming environment. Start with a clean, tidy space. Then, add some seasonal decor. Think about using autumn leaves, pumpkins, or candles.

2. **Use Soft Lighting**
   Lighting can set the mood. Instead of harsh overhead lights, use soft lighting to create a cozy atmosphere. Use table lamps, string lights, or even candles. Dimmed lights help everyone feel relaxed and comfortable.

3. **Arrange Comfortable Seating**
   Ensure there's plenty of comfortable seating for everyone. Arrange chairs and couches so that people can chat easily. You want guests to feel invited to sit down and enjoy each other's

company.

4. **Add Personal Touches**

   Personal touches go a long way. Display family photos or artwork that reflects your style. A small guest book where people can write a note or share a memory can also be a lovely addition. It encourages guests to engage with one another.

5. **Set Up a Welcoming Entryway**

   The entryway is the first impression. Make it inviting. A clean space, a warm welcome mat, and a coat rack can make your guests feel at home. Add a little sign that says "Welcome" to set the tone.

6. **Consider Background Music**

   Soft background music can enhance the atmosphere. Choose something light and cheerful. Instrumental music or classic tunes can create a relaxed vibe without overwhelming conversations. Keep the volume low to encourage chatting.

Engaging Guests in Activities

While you prepare the meal, it's important to keep your guests entertained. Here are some low-pressure activities that everyone can enjoy.

1. **Icebreaker Games**

   Start with simple icebreaker games to help guests mingle. A fun game like "Two Truths and a Lie" is a great way to get everyone talking. Each person shares two true facts and one false one. Others guess which is the lie. It's a light-hearted way to spark conversations.

2. **Create a Gratitude Tree**

   Set up a gratitude tree. Provide small pieces of paper and pens. Encourage guests to write down what they're thankful for and hang their notes on the tree. This activity fosters connection and reflection. Plus, it makes for a lovely decoration!

3. **Cooking Together**

   If your guests are up for it, invite them to join in the cooking. It's a fun way to bond. Assign simple tasks like chopping vegetables or stirring a pot. This not only helps you but also creates a collaborative atmosphere.

4. **Board Games or Card Games**

   Have some board games or cards on hand. These can be great for keeping guests entertained. Choose games that are easy to learn and suitable for all ages. It's a relaxed way for everyone to interact and have fun.

5. **Story Sharing**

   Encourage guests to share stories or memories. This can be about past Thanksgivings or fun family tales. It's a great way to connect and often leads to laughter. Plus, it can make your gathering feel more intimate.

6. **Outdoor Activities**

   If the weather permits, consider outdoor activities. A game of catch, a walk around the neighborhood, or even a quick hike can be refreshing. It's a great way to get some fresh air and enjoy nature together.

Handling Unexpected Situations Gracefully

No matter how well you plan, surprises can happen. Here's how to manage unexpected situations with ease.

1. **Last-Minute Guests**

   Sometimes, unexpected guests arrive. Stay calm if this happens. Have extra chairs and plates ready for such occasions. A little extra food is usually easy to prepare or add to your meal. Simply welcome them warmly and include them in the fun.

2. **Forgotten Dishes**

If someone forgets to bring a dish, don't panic. Check what you have on hand. You might have ingredients to whip up something quick. A simple salad or extra bread can be made in minutes. Or, if possible, ask someone to run to the store for a last-minute purchase.

3. **Changes in Plans**

   Changes in plans can throw you off. If the turkey takes longer to cook, that's okay! Adjust your schedule. Keep guests updated and involve them in making new plans. Staying flexible and positive will help everyone relax.

4. **Technical Difficulties**

   Technology can fail us. If the music stops playing or the TV isn't working for the big game, don't worry. Instead, engage your guests in conversation or suggest a game. This keeps the mood light and fun, regardless of tech issues.

5. **Tension Among Guests**

   Occasionally, tensions can rise among guests. If you sense any awkwardness, try to diffuse the situation. Change the subject or engage others in conversation. Keep the focus on positive topics and shared experiences.

6. **Self-Care**

   Lastly, don't forget to take care of yourself. Hosting can be exhausting. Take short breaks when needed. Step outside for some fresh air or grab a drink. Keeping yourself calm helps everyone else feel at ease.

Wrapping Up

Hosting Thanksgiving doesn't have to be stressful. By creating a warm atmosphere, engaging your guests, and managing unexpected situations gracefully, you can enjoy the day to its fullest.

Focus on making everyone feel welcome and connected. Remember, the heart of Thanksgiving is not just about the food but about the people you share it with. Enjoy the laughter, the conversations, and the love that fills your home.

So, get ready to host with ease! With these tips, you'll create wonderful memories that will last a lifetime. Happy Thanksgiving!

Chapter 8

Thanksgiving is a time for family. It can also be a time for tension. Different personalities, past conflicts, and strong opinions can lead to disagreements. But with a little preparation, you can navigate these challenges gracefully. This chapter will offer practical tips for handling family dynamics, keeping conversations positive, and fostering gratitude and connection.

Preparing for Family Tension

Understanding that family tension can happen is the first step. Here are some practical tips to help you prepare.

1. **Acknowledge Past Conflicts**
   If there have been past disagreements, acknowledge them. Ignoring issues won't make them disappear. If you know certain topics trigger arguments, plan ahead. Consider addressing them calmly before the gathering. A simple conversation can help set expectations for the day.

2. **Set Ground Rules**
   Before dinner, it might be helpful to set some ground rules. Let your guests know that certain topics are off-limits. This can include politics, religion, or any sensitive subjects. Clear guidelines can help everyone feel more comfortable.

3. **Be a Good Listener**
   When conflicts arise, be ready to listen. Sometimes, all a person needs is to feel heard. Validate their feelings, even if you don't

agree. Acknowledging someone's perspective can go a long way in diffusing tension.

4. **Stay Calm and Collected**

Your demeanor sets the tone for the gathering. If you remain calm, others are likely to follow suit. If a disagreement arises, take a deep breath. Responding instead of reacting can prevent escalation. Keep your voice steady and your tone light.

5. **Have an Exit Strategy**

In case tensions rise, it's good to have a plan. If a conversation gets heated, suggest a quick break. You could step outside for fresh air or help in the kitchen. Taking a moment to regroup can help everyone cool down.

6. **Encourage Teamwork**

Encourage family members to work together. Assign tasks that require cooperation. This can be setting the table or preparing a dish together. Working as a team can strengthen bonds and create positive interactions.

Keeping Conversations Light and Positive

Keeping conversations light can prevent tension from escalating. Here are some ways to steer discussions in a positive direction.

1. **Start with Icebreakers**

Begin dinner with light-hearted icebreaker questions. Ask everyone to share their favorite Thanksgiving memory. This helps set a positive tone and encourages sharing fun stories.

2. **Focus on Fun Topics**

Steer conversations toward fun and neutral topics. Consider discussing holiday plans, favorite recipes, or funny family stories. These subjects can keep everyone engaged without diving into divisive issues.

3. **Avoid Divisive Subjects**

If a sensitive topic arises, gently redirect the conversation. For instance, if politics come up, you could say, "Let's talk about something more fun. What's everyone's favorite holiday movie?" This shift can lighten the mood and bring smiles.

4. **Use Humor**

   A good laugh can diffuse tension. Share light-hearted jokes or funny anecdotes from past Thanksgivings. Humor creates a relaxed atmosphere and helps everyone bond.

5. **Encourage Gratitude Sharing**

   Invite everyone to share what they are thankful for. This can be a wonderful way to focus on positive aspects of life. You can even go around the table, giving each person a chance to speak. This creates a sense of unity and appreciation.

6. **Create a "Gratitude Jar"**

   Set up a gratitude jar where guests can write down what they're thankful for on slips of paper. Encourage them to share their notes throughout the meal. This activity promotes reflection and connection.

Focusing on Gratitude and Connection

Gratitude and connection are at the heart of Thanksgiving. Here's how to encourage these values despite any family tension.

1. **Lead by Example**

   Show gratitude through your actions. Thank your guests for coming and express appreciation for their presence. Your positive attitude can inspire others to follow suit.

2. **Create a Gratitude Table Setting**

   Consider adding elements that symbolize gratitude to your table setting. Place a small flower arrangement or candles to create a warm atmosphere. You could also have place cards with each guest's name and a positive note about them. This encourages appreciation.

3. **Highlight Shared Experiences**

   Remind everyone of the shared experiences that bring them together. Whether it's family traditions or childhood memories, highlighting these connections fosters a sense of unity. This can remind everyone of the love that exists despite differences.

4. **Plan Group Activities**

   Incorporate group activities that encourage bonding. A fun game, a group walk, or even a family photo session can strengthen connections. These activities help everyone engage and create lasting memories.

5. **Express Affection**

   Don't shy away from expressing love and affection. Hugs, smiles, and warm words can create a welcoming environment. This reinforces the idea that family matters, even during tough times.

6. **Reflect Together**

   At the end of the meal, take a moment to reflect. Ask everyone to share their favorite part of the day or what they appreciated most. This reflection promotes connection and gratitude.

Wrapping Up

Thanksgiving is a special time to gather with family. While tensions can arise, preparing for them can make a significant difference. By acknowledging conflicts, keeping conversations light, and focusing on gratitude, you can create a warm and inviting atmosphere.

Remember, the goal is connection. Embrace the spirit of Thanksgiving by fostering love and appreciation. With these strategies, you'll navigate family dynamics with grace. Enjoy the laughter, the stories, and the time spent together. Happy Thanksgiving!

Chapter 9

Thanksgiving dinner is a beautiful experience. You've spent hours preparing, cooking, and sharing food with family and friends. After the last bite, it's time to shift gears. The focus now is on relaxing and reflecting. This chapter will help you simplify clean-up, create a relaxing post-dinner environment, and take a moment to appreciate the day.

Simplifying Clean-Up

After a festive meal, clean-up can feel overwhelming. But it doesn't have to be. Here are some tips to make it easier and more efficient.

1. **Set the Stage Early**
   Before your guests arrive, set up a clean-up station. Place garbage bags and recycling bins in easy-to-reach spots. This encourages everyone to toss their waste as they finish eating. A little organization goes a long way.

2. **Enlist Help**
   Don't be afraid to ask for help. Most guests are happy to lend a hand. Delegate tasks like clearing plates, wiping the table, or washing dishes. This not only speeds up the process but also fosters a sense of teamwork.

3. **Use Disposable Dishes**
   If you want a truly stress-free clean-up, consider using disposable plates and utensils. While they may not be the most eco-friendly option, they can save time and effort. Just remember to have enough trash bags on hand for easy disposal.

4. **Clean As You Go**

   Encourage a clean-as-you-go approach during the meal. As guests finish their dishes, have them stack their plates and cups. This keeps things tidy and prevents a massive pile-up after dinner.

5. **Do a Quick Tidy-Up**

   After the meal, take a few minutes for a quick tidy-up. Clear the dining table and remove any leftovers. Place them in containers for later. This will create a clean space for the next part of the evening.

6. **Create a Dishwasher Assembly Line**

   If you have a dishwasher, set up an assembly line. One person can load while another rinses. This system speeds up the process and makes it more fun. Plus, it allows everyone to chat while they work.

7. **Plan for Leftovers**

   Have containers ready for leftovers. Label them for easy identification. This will save you time later in the week. Guests can also take home a meal, which is always appreciated.

8. **Play Some Music**

   While cleaning up, put on some upbeat music. This helps lighten the mood and makes the task feel less tedious. Singing along or dancing a little can turn clean-up into a mini-party.

9. **Set a Timer**

   Give yourself a set time to clean up. For example, say you'll spend 20 minutes tidying up. When the timer goes off, you can take a break. This helps keep everyone focused and motivated.

10. **Reward Yourself**

    After clean-up, treat yourself to a small reward. Enjoy a slice of pie or a cup of tea. Acknowledge your hard work and let yourself relax.

Creating a Relaxing Post-Dinner Environment

After the meal, it's essential to create a calm and inviting atmosphere. Here are some ideas to help you unwind and enjoy the rest of the evening.

1. **Dim the Lights**

   Lower the lights to create a cozy ambiance. This signals that it's time to relax. Use soft lamps or candles to add warmth to the room. The right lighting sets the mood for the evening.

2. **Serve Comforting Drinks**

   After dinner, consider offering warm drinks. Hot cocoa, cider, or herbal tea can help guests unwind. Provide a cozy beverage station where people can help themselves.

3. **Set Up a Movie Area**

   If your family enjoys watching movies, set up a cozy area for a film. Bring out blankets and cushions. Select a light-hearted movie or a holiday classic to keep the mood joyful.

4. **Organize Games**

   Board games or card games can be a fun way to spend time together. Choose games that are easy to understand and don't require too much setup. This keeps everyone engaged without stress.

5. **Create a Conversation Corner**

   Arrange a comfortable seating area for chatting. Encourage guests to gather for conversation. This relaxed setting allows for meaningful discussions and laughter.

6. **Play Soft Background Music**

   After the meal, switch to softer background music. Instrumental music or gentle holiday tunes can create a calming atmosphere. It helps everyone feel at ease.

7. **Encourage Guests to Share Stories**

   Invite guests to share their favorite Thanksgiving memories or family stories. This fosters connection and creates a sense of belonging. Everyone loves a good story.

8. **Take a Family Photo**

   Capture the moment by taking a family photo after dinner. Gather everyone for a quick snapshot. This creates a lasting memory and a fun keepsake for all.

9. **Provide Cozy Blankets**

   Keep a few cozy blankets nearby. Guests may appreciate snuggling up as the evening progresses. This adds to the relaxed vibe and makes everyone feel at home.

10. **Plan for Some Quiet Time**

    After a busy day, it's okay to have some quiet time. Encourage guests to relax and reflect. Whether it's reading a book or enjoying some peace, it's important to recharge.

Reflecting on the Day with Gratitude

Once the clean-up is done and the atmosphere is relaxed, take a moment to reflect. Thanksgiving is about gratitude and connection. Here's how to embrace these values after the meal.

1. **Gather in a Circle**

   If it feels right, gather everyone in a circle. This creates an intimate setting for sharing. You can encourage everyone to express what they are thankful for that day.

2. **Keep It Light**

   Remember, this is a time for positivity. Encourage sharing lighthearted moments or funny mishaps from the day. Laughter is an excellent way to reflect on the joy of the occasion.

3. **Write It Down**

   Consider keeping a gratitude journal. After Thanksgiving, write down your reflections on the day. Capture the moments that brought you joy. This practice can help reinforce a positive mindset.

4. **Share Specifics**

When reflecting, encourage guests to be specific. Instead of saying, "I'm thankful for family," they might say, "I'm thankful for the way Aunt Lucy made us laugh today." This adds depth to the gratitude shared.

5. **Express Your Thanks**

Take a moment to express your appreciation for your guests. Thank them for coming and for being part of the day. A little kindness goes a long way.

6. **Focus on the Connections Made**

Instead of dwelling on what didn't go perfectly, focus on the connections made. The smiles, the laughter, and the love shared are what truly matter. Reflecting on these moments fosters a sense of fulfillment.

7. **Encourage Future Gatherings**

As you reflect, discuss future gatherings. Express excitement for the next holiday or family event. This keeps the spirit of togetherness alive and encourages plans for the future.

8. **Plan a Thank You**

Consider planning a follow-up thank you. Sending a card or a message to your guests shows your appreciation. It reinforces the connections made and keeps the gratitude flowing.

9. **Capture the Moments**

If you took photos throughout the day, share them with your guests. You could create a shared album or send them individual photos. This helps everyone relive the special moments.

10. **End on a Positive Note**

As the evening winds down, end on a positive note. Whether it's sharing a final toast or a warm goodbye, make it memorable.

This leaves everyone feeling good about the day.

Wrapping Up

The time after the meal is just as important as the meal itself. By simplifying clean-up, creating a relaxing environment, and reflecting on the day, you can transition into a peaceful evening.

Remember, Thanksgiving is about connection, gratitude, and love. Embrace these values as the day comes to a close. Enjoy the laughter, the stories, and the warmth of being together. Happy Thanksgiving!

Chapter 10

Thanksgiving is a time for family, friends, and food. It's also a chance to create memories and traditions. However, traditions can sometimes feel like a chore. This chapter will help you build meaningful Thanksgiving traditions that bring joy, not stress. We'll explore choosing traditions, letting go of what doesn't work, and focusing on gratitude year-round.

Choosing Meaningful Traditions

Traditions should enhance your Thanksgiving experience. They should be fun and meaningful. Here's how to choose traditions that work for you.

1. **Reflect on What Matters**
   Start by thinking about what you love about Thanksgiving. Is it food, family, or fun activities? Reflecting on what brings you joy helps you find traditions that matter.

2. **Involve Everyone**
   Talk to your family about their favorite Thanksgiving memories. Ask them what traditions they love or want to start. Involving everyone makes the experience more inclusive.

3. **Keep It Simple**
   Traditions don't have to be elaborate. Sometimes the simplest traditions are the most meaningful. A family walk after dinner or playing a game can create lasting memories.

4. **Try Something New**
   If you feel stuck in a rut, consider trying something new. It

could be a new recipe, a different activity, or even a theme for the day. Trying new things can keep the spirit of Thanksgiving fresh.

5. **Create a Family Recipe Book**

   Start a family recipe book. Gather favorite recipes from each family member. This tradition can grow over the years and become a cherished keepsake. Each Thanksgiving, you can add a new recipe.

6. **Establish a Gratitude Jar**

   Create a gratitude jar for your family. Have everyone write down what they are thankful for each year. On Thanksgiving, read them together. This simple tradition encourages reflection and appreciation.

7. **Volunteer Together**

   Consider volunteering as a family on or before Thanksgiving. Helping those in need can strengthen your bond and remind everyone of the spirit of giving. It's a beautiful way to celebrate together.

8. **Start a Thanksgiving Storytelling Time**

   Designate time for storytelling. Family members can share their favorite Thanksgiving stories or memories. This tradition helps everyone connect and keeps the focus on the holiday's essence.

9. **Capture the Day with Photos**

   Make it a tradition to take photos every Thanksgiving. Capture candid moments, posed family pictures, and even funny ones. Create an album to look back on in years to come.

10. **Celebrate with Friends**

    If you have friends who feel like family, invite them to join your Thanksgiving. Blending traditions from different families can create a rich and diverse experience. It's a great way to share love and laughter.

Letting Go of Unnecessary Pressure

Not every tradition needs to continue. Sometimes traditions can become burdensome. Here's how to let go of what doesn't serve your family.

1. **Assess Your Traditions**

   Take a look at your current traditions. Ask yourself if they bring joy or stress. If something feels like a chore, it might be time to rethink it.

2. **Communicate Openly**

   Talk to your family about which traditions feel burdensome. Open communication allows everyone to express their feelings. This helps everyone feel heard and understood.

3. **Be Honest About Time and Resources**

   Consider your time and resources when evaluating traditions. If a tradition requires too much effort or money, it may need to change. Prioritize what truly matters to your family.

4. **Adapt Traditions**

   Instead of dropping a tradition entirely, consider adapting it. Can a complex recipe be simplified? Could an event be made shorter? Finding ways to adapt can help maintain the spirit without stress.

5. **Choose Quality Over Quantity**

   Focus on a few meaningful traditions rather than trying to do everything. Quality experiences are more memorable than numerous events that feel forced.

6. **Let Go of Perfection**

   Remember that Thanksgiving doesn't have to be perfect. It's okay if things don't go as planned. Embrace the messiness of family gatherings. Those imperfect moments often lead to the best memories.

7. **Create Flexibility**

   Allow flexibility in your traditions. If one feels hectic, it's okay to skip or modify a tradition. Life changes, and your traditions can evolve with it.

8. **Don't Feel Guilty**

   Letting go of traditions that no longer serve you can feel guilt-inducing. Remember, it's okay to prioritize your family's well-being. Traditions should enhance your experience, not weigh it down.

9. **Encourage New Traditions**

   If a tradition no longer works, encourage the idea of creating new ones. This can be exciting and liberating. New traditions can bring fresh energy to your Thanksgiving celebrations.

10. **Celebrate Small Wins**

    Even if you drop a tradition, find ways to celebrate small wins. Acknowledge what you and your family do well together. Every moment of joy counts, regardless of tradition.

Focusing on Gratitude Year-Round

Thanksgiving is often associated with gratitude, but why limit it to just one day? Here's how to carry the spirit of Thanksgiving beyond the holiday.

1. **Practice Daily Gratitude**

   Encourage your family to express gratitude daily. This could be a simple morning or evening routine. Each family member can share one thing they are thankful for.

2. **Start a Gratitude Journal**

   Keep a gratitude journal as a family. Write down things you are thankful for each week. Reflecting regularly can deepen your appreciation for everyday moments.

3. **Celebrate Gratitude Days**

   Choose a day each month to celebrate gratitude. It could be a small gathering, a special meal, or a family activity focused on giving thanks.

4. **Create Gratitude Rituals**
   Develop rituals around gratitude. Light a candle or say a prayer before meals. These rituals can remind everyone to pause and appreciate what they have.

5. **Volunteer Regularly**
   Make volunteering a regular activity. Choose a cause that matters to your family. This reinforces the importance of giving back and appreciating what you have.

6. **Share Thankfulness with Others**
   Encourage your family to express gratitude to others. This could be writing thank-you notes or making phone calls to friends and family. Sharing appreciation can strengthen bonds.

7. **Discuss Gratitude in Tough Times**
   Talk about gratitude during difficult moments. Discussing what you're thankful for, even in tough situations, can help shift perspectives. It builds resilience and fosters a positive outlook.

8. **Incorporate Gratitude into Family Traditions**
   Weave gratitude into existing family traditions. For example, during holiday gatherings, make it a point to share what you're thankful for that year.

9. **Practice Mindfulness**
   Encourage mindfulness practices that focus on gratitude. Whether it's meditation or simply taking a moment to breathe, these practices can deepen your appreciation for life's simple pleasures.

10. **Celebrate Milestones with Gratitude**
    Acknowledge milestones throughout the year. Birthdays, anniversaries, and achievements are perfect opportunities to express gratitude. Celebrate together as a family to reinforce the spirit of appreciation.

Wrapping Up

Thanksgiving is about more than just one day. It's time to create traditions that matter. Focus on what brings joy and let go of what causes stress. Carry the spirit of gratitude throughout the year.

Building Thanksgiving traditions without the stress is achievable. With thoughtful planning and open communication, you can create lasting memories. Embrace the joy of togetherness and cherish each moment. After all, Thanksgiving is about love, laughter, and being thankful for the gift of family.

Continue your journey with a stress-free Christmas with *A Calm Christmas.*

Also by Karen Kazimer Shockley

Hearts United
Hearts United in Faith
Hearts United In Love
Hearts United in Love
Hearts United In Celebration

Write. Publish. Thrive.
Secrets of Writing & Publishing

Standalone
Stress-Free Thanksgiving

Watch for more at https://karens-words.mailchimpsites.com.

About the Author

Karen Kazimer Shockley was raised with an almost overwhelming amount of religious exposure. Karen began a journey to use this information to bring religion to a place where it was real in her life. This process reached critical mass when she met a wonderful man who embodied the true Christian life, without structured religion. Through his influence, she began to recognize spiritual presences in her own life. Her goal is to share these experiences with others so that they, too, can continue their journey to spiritual peace.

Read more at https://karens-words.mailchimpsites.com/.